This Page Left Intentionally Blank

TABLE OF CONTENTS

This Page Left Intentionally Blank

The June 2013 U.S. Navy-U.S. Coast Guard National Fleet Policy statement, *The National Fleet: A Joint United States Navy and United States Coast Guard*, directed the production of this National Fleet Plan. It is intended to identify opportunities to increase the commonality and interoperability of Navy and Coast Guard forces and better enable the two components to operate together in support of their mutual homeland security and national defense missions. In this document, the Navy and Coast Guard have identified authorities, methods, and measurements to achieve efficiency and effectiveness, and jointly developed plans of action and milestones in the following areas:

- Current and evolving operations
- Integrated logistics
- Training
- Command, control, communications systems
- Sensors
- Engineering systems
- Weapons systems
- Platforms

In support of the *U.S. National Strategy for Maritime Security* and the Sea Service's *Cooperative Strategy for 21st Century Sea Power*, the Navy and Coast Guard will implement the actions in this Plan. The National Fleet Board, through established Commonality Working Groups, will monitor the progress of the Plan's actions and provide periodic assessment reports. As the maritime environment changes over time, we will serve as good stewards of our constrained resources and adjust this Plan at our annual Navy-Coast Guard Staff Talks.

As we noted in our National Fleet Policy, "The Navy and Coast Guard best serve the Nation when we deliberately prepare our forces for integrated naval and maritime operations." Today, the Navy and Coast Guard plan and operate together as the world's premier maritime services. This Plan will assure flexible, adaptable, and capable forces best suited to the complex maritime environment of the future, vital to the continued security of the United States.

Jonathan W. Greenert	Robert J. Papp, Jr.
Admiral, Unite States Navy	Admiral, United States Coast Guard
Chief of Naval Operations	Commandant of the Coast Guard

1. <u>PREAMBLE</u>. The June 2013 Chief of Naval Operations and Commandant of the United States Coast Guard's joint policy statement, *The National Fleet: A Joint United States Navy and United States Coast Guard*, referred to hereafter as the "National Fleet Policy," directs the Navy and Coast Guard to achieve commonality and interoperability for 21st century maritime and naval operations. This commonality and interoperability is intended to ensure effective and efficient operations when Navy and Coast Guard forces mutually support each other. In response to, and as directed by the National Fleet Policy, this National Fleet Plan, hereafter, "The Plan," provides the detailed action and milestones both will implement to reach those objectives.

2. <u>PURPOSE</u>. Given the complexity and lethality of national security threats in the maritime domain, and in support of the *U.S. National Strategy for Maritime Security*, and the Sea Service's (Navy, Marine Corps, and Coast Guard) joint maritime strategy, *A Cooperative Strategy for 21st Century Sea Power*, it is vital to America's interests that the Navy and Coast Guard collaboratively plan, field, and sustain interoperable and affordable forces to provide complementary, non-redundant support for each other's mission sets. As good stewards of the Nation's resources and faced with an uncertain budget environment, it is imperative that our services cooperate in a deliberate manner. Implementation of the National Fleet Policy will provide the Nation with more interoperable and fiscally efficient Navy and Coast Guard forces.

The National Fleet Plan identifies specific Navy and Coast Guard authorities, methods, and measurements to avoid redundancies and achieve economies of scale. It improves operational effectiveness and provides a mechanism to enhance integration and resource development. The Plan is adaptive to meet emerging national security threats and scalable to address changing service challenges.

3. <u>NATIONAL FLEET PLAN OVERVIEW</u>. The National Fleet Policy and Charter of the National Fleet Board directed the establishment of a Flag-Level Board consisting of six Navy and six Coast Guard officers from the staffs of the Office of the Chief of Naval Operations (OPNAV) and Coast Guard Headquarters. The Board is co-chaired by the OPNAV Director, Strategy and Policy Division (OPNAV N51) and the Coast Guard's Assistant Commandant for Response Policy (CG-5R), reporting to both the OPNAV Deputy Chief of Naval Operations for Operations, Plans, and Strategy (OPNAV N3/N5) and the Deputy Commandant for Operations (CG-DCO) .

As directed, the National Fleet Plan is tasked to:

a. Identify potential opportunities to increase the commonality and interoperability of the National Fleet. Specifically focus on platforms, equipment, weapons and weapons systems, material, supplies, facilities, maintenance, and supporting services. Additionally, determine and identify the equipment and material to be procured or developed, training and certifications required to prepare for missions and integrated operations, and the operation of our supply/logistics systems.

b. Examine Navy and Coast Guard logistics processes and integration initiatives; research and development; acquisitions; information and intelligence systems integration; force planning; resourcing; procurement; doctrine development; training; exercises; and operational planning processes to further develop mutually supporting forces.

c. Validate Navy and Coast Guard specific and non-redundant warfighting capability requirements to ensure both services are poised to meet current and emerging threats to national security during times of peace and war through deliberate design and acquisition processes.

4. <u>PLAN PROGRESSION AND OVERSIGHT</u>. As directed by its Charter, the National Fleet Board will provide review and oversight of the Plan's implementation and progress. The Board Co-Chairs will receive periodic updates from the leads of the Commonality Working Groups and report the status of the Plan and its progress, along with an annual Plan update for signature, to the Chief of Naval Operations and the Commandant of the Coast Guard at the annual Navy-Coast Guard Staff Talks. In conjunction with the annual review, the Board Co-Chairs will update the list of effective Memoranda of Agreement/Understanding (Section 8) and the list of established Commonality Working Groups in the National Fleet Board Charter.

5. <u>NATIONAL FLEET PLAN</u>.

5.1 CURRENT AND EVOLVING OPERATIONS.

a. INTRODUCTION. Current operations and associated service-level planning efforts focus on processes, policy, and mutually beneficial relationships to ensure mission success. Continuous innovation and adaptation by the Navy and Coast Guard inform a forward-looking effort to describe ways to enhance our joint capabilities to address emerging threats. Our globally-distributed, mission-tailored forces contribute to homeland defense in depth and provide the basis for a secure maritime environment. As our interoperable forces continue to coalesce, we bring a robust blend of "hard" and "soft" power and a range of military options in support of national objectives and enduring national interests. The synergy generated from our ability to plan collaboratively and our proven experience operating together yield great benefits for security, stability, and crisis response. The Navy and Coast Guard are uniquely postured to conduct cooperative international engagement in the maritime domain while building broad partnerships across a range of mission areas.

Navy and Coast Guard forces maintain a symbiotic relationship that benefits the nation as a whole. This relationship is most noticeable during ongoing operations, but it starts with conceptualization, continues through the planning cycle, and culminates during mission execution. In the near-term (today through FY18), Navy and Coast Guard will prioritize the actionable initiatives below to improve commonality and interoperability.

b. CURRENT STATE (FY14 to FY18).

1) Improve Arctic capabilities. The opening of the Arctic will present the Navy and Coast Guard team with new challenges to ensure freedom of navigation, support search and rescue efforts, and maintain maritime security. The May 2013 *U.S. National Strategy for the Arctic Region*, along with the November 2013 DoD Arctic Strategy, the *United States Coast Guard's Arctic Strategy* and the *U.S. Navy Arctic Roadmap*, describe how we will approach these challenges and opportunities by advancing our security interests, pursuing responsible Arctic stewardship, and strengthening international cooperation. The Navy and Coast Guard will continue to have a role maintaining safety and security in the harsh environment as changing ice conditions enable economic opportunities and with that, some level of increased human activity. Mutually supporting relationships will be essential for carrying out distinct service mission sets that require specialized equipment, training, logistics and a heightened level of interoperability. Enduring reviews of requirements and capabilities, coupled with a shared understanding of roles will enable the services to shape programs and operations.

The issues confronted by both services are best analyzed when viewed through a common lens. Formation of a USN/USCG Arctic Working Group will codify relationships and assist in aligning strategies, policies, and capabilities needed to address the challenges of the region.

2) Continue to employ and refine adaptive force packaging. Adaptive force packaging provides commanders with flexible resources that bring additional capabilities and authorities to meet mission specific objectives. Beyond innovatively integrating ships or aircraft into task forces, adaptive force packaging incorporates transferable crew and equipment modules to meet demands and enhance effectiveness. It directly supports the Sea Service's goal of globally distributed-mission tailored maritime forces.

Navy and Coast Guard forces routinely deploy together to conduct Counter-Illicit Trafficking (CIT) operations, Counter-Piracy (CP) missions, Maritime Interception Operations (MIO) and Theater Security Cooperation (TSC) missions around the globe. Visit, Board, Search, and Seizure (VBSS) teams and integrated units must continuously refine tactics, techniques, and procedures in order to meet evolving threats. To effectively provide tailored capabilities and authorities, joint USN/USCG forces must fully comprehend the skills and limitations available, and understand the terms of reference commonly used during operations.

3) Advance National efforts to enhance Maritime Domain Awareness (MDA). In December 2013, the National Security Staff released the National Maritime Domain Awareness Plan (NMDAP) to provide a National focus on MDA in support of homeland defense. A supporting plan for the U.S. National Strategy for Maritime Security, the NMDAP promotes global maritime security through improved understanding of the full spectrum of activity in the maritime domain. It promotes

8

favorable conditions for information sharing and synthesis, including intelligence information, to better inform decisions affecting the security, safety, economy, and environment of the maritime commons. Navy and Coast Guard will address the MDA challenges identified in the NMDAP by improving information sharing; emphasizing the use of common data standards and collaborative information environments; and fostering partnerships with international and interagency partners.

4) <u>Integrate Homeland Missions/Interagency Operations Centers</u>. Navy and Coast Guard units and operations centers within the United States must continue to support information sharing, collaborative planning, and coordination of operations. Shared situational awareness through common (user-defined) maritime pictures across Combatant Command, Navy and Coast Guard Operations and Fusion Centers is an essential component of operational decision making and integrated maritime operations. We must be able to efficiently sustain operations such as high value unit (HVU) protection and seamlessly transition to on-demand response operations to counter threats to the homeland. Interoperable units such as Coast Guard Marine Force Protection Units charged with protecting ballistic missile submarines provide an excellent example of integration including shared platforms, doctrine and planning.

5) <u>Share Liaison Officers (LNOs)</u>. The Coast Guard currently has three officers assigned to the Pentagon to work directly with the Navy on matters of mutual interest. Those officers are assigned to OPNAV N2/N6F Warfare Integration, OPNAV N3/N5 Operations, Plans and Strategy, and N96 Surface Warfare. There are additional personnel exchanges on Echelon II/III staffs (e.g., Naval Air Systems Command (NAVAIR) Liaison Officer at CGHQ advises/coordinates NAVAIR support for USCG aviation acquisition, engineering and cutter aviation facility certification efforts.) Liaison officers between the naval services act as valuable communication nodes and serve as conduits for articulating service priorities in addition to duties that directly influence planning and operations.

5.2 INTEGRATED LOGISTICS.

a. INTRODUCTION.

1) Effective teamwork by the Navy and Coast Guard in both naval and joint warfighting environments requires integrated logistics processes. Both services, through the Naval Logistics Integration Enterprise and other forums, actively pursue appropriate courses of action to improve naval logistics to the fullest extent possible by integrating service logistics capabilities and capacities. The overarching goals of integrating logistics are to:

a) Increase commonality with Navy and Coast Guard logistics doctrine, business processes, technologies, and systems to optimize logistics performance in support of future operations.

b) Better connect Navy and Coast Guard logistics organizations and strengthen professional development to enhance support of expeditionary forces.

2) Integrating logistics throughout the Navy and Coast Guard can produce significant savings and help improve support to the warfighter. Expected outcomes and benefits include:

   a) Improved logistics responsiveness and agility to better support the warfighter and increase resiliency.

   b) Improved and sustained combat support readiness.

   c) Improved efficiency through reduced logistics workload afloat and ashore.

   d) Reevaluation of naval logistics processes for more efficient use of resources.

   e) Identify common processes between the Services to improve support to the warfighter, eliminate unnecessary duplication, and enhance sustainability.

3) Specific areas of Navy and Coast Guard integrated logistics efforts include supply chain management, common parts identification, inventory management, requisition management, asset visibility, warehousing, fueling, maintenance, facilities integration, and training. The longstanding Naval Logistics Integration (NLI) Enterprise and the Defense Logistics Agency (DLA) Partnership Council address many of these topics.

b. CURRENT STATE (FY14 to FY18).

   1) USN/USCG working groups identifying commonality of parts between USCG National Security Cutter (NSC) and USN Littoral Combat Ship (LCS). (NLI)

      a) Identification of Common Systems.
      b) Commonality of Spares.
      c) Provisioning/Supply Support.
      d) Training.

   2) Incorporating the USCG Offshore Patrol Cutter (OPC) and USN Joint High Speed Vessel (JHSV) into the NLI NSC/LCS commonality effort. (NLI)

   3) Utilize DLA as a responsive and cost effective source of supply for parts for additional Coast Guard unique assets (i.e., 110' Coastal Patrol Cutters), a follow-on to the 87' Coastal Patrol Cutter parts inventory already managed by DLA. Identifying additional Coast Guard parts carried by DLA will potentially identify additional parts commonality with USN items.

4) Explore opportunities to consolidate warehousing locations with USN/USMC/DLA sites. (NLI & DLA)

5) Assess additional opportunities to share fuel stocks, develop common payment methods and research/test bio-fuels with USN/DLA. (DLA)

6) A joint USCG/USN/USMC VBSS Working Group identifies areas to standardize VBSS equipment.

7) Coast Guard Transit Protection System (TPS) escorts utilize the Navy supply system to acquire parts for the weapons systems and Arms, Ammunition and Explosives (AA&E) lockers.

8) Potential consolidation opportunities exist for Coastal Riverine Force (USN)/Port Security Unit (USCG) equipment.

9) The Services are jointly developing a TPS Integrated Logistics Support Plan (ILSP) with the intent of consolidating existing Life Cycle Support plans and agreements.

10) Coordinating maintenance and readiness sustainment work between the Coast Guard's Surface Forces Logistics Center (SFLC) and the Naval Systems Commands (NAVAIR, Naval Sea Systems Command (NAVSEA), Space and Naval Warfare Systems Command (SPAWAR)) with respect to casualty reporting and responses associated with Navy Type-Navy Owned (NTNO) weapons systems.

11) USCG use of the Navy Working Uniform (NWU) Type II in support of Naval Special Warfare.

12) Common logistics solutions to support arctic operations.

   a) Integrated operational logistics planning in support of USN/USCG operations above the Arctic Circle.
   b) Conduct a comprehensive logistics capabilities review to determine opportunities for Arctic logistics integration.

13) Class II individual combat clothing and equipment commonality.

   a) Streamline RDT&E (Research, Development, Test and Evaluation), acquisition, and supply chain management for common items.
   b) USN and USCG coordinate with USMC who has responsibility for the procurement of selected Class II items (specifically, individual ballistic protection systems, individual load bearing systems, flame resistant gear and cold weather gear) for all naval expeditionary forces.

14) Common logistics solutions to support USN C-130 and USCG HC-130 operations.

c. FUTURE STATE (FY19 to FY23).

1) Assess remaining Coast Guard inventory items for induction into DLA systems.

2) Identify requirements for establishing a logistics support infrastructure in the Arctic.

3) Identify potential information technology solutions for sharing common asset visibility between services.

4) Identify potential information technology solutions for sharing platform configuration management information between services.

5) Identify requirements and potentially award common maintenance support contracts for LCS/NSC/OPC.

6) Develop mechanisms and business rules to share common Depot Level Repairable (DLR) inventory between the Services.

5.3 TRAINING.

a. INTRODUCTION. This section of the National Fleet Plan consists of individual/specialized skills training and fleet training engagements, operations, and exercises between the Navy and Coast Guard. It includes detail on shared courses of instruction and current and enduring fleet opportunities. Other areas of discussion include existing USN-USCG Commonality Working Groups, potential initiatives for increased interoperability training and engagement, future initiatives, and estimated timelines to achieve these efforts.

b. CURRENT STATE (FY14 to FY18).

1) Individual/Specialized Skills Training:

   a) Average annual USCG throughput at Navy schoolhouses ranges from 2000-2500 students in over 200 formal Navy courses.
   b) Navy courses are managed and delivered by ten Fleet commands or warfare enterprises, seven Naval Education and Training Command (NETC) Learning Centers, and two non-NETC training commands.
   c) Coast Guard schoolhouses reserve and graduate approximately 120-140 seats for Navy students on an annual basis in eight formal Coast Guard courses.
   d) Coast Guard courses are managed by Force Readiness Command and delivered at four Coast Guard Training Centers and via exportable training teams.
   e) Total combined Navy and Coast Guard Courses include:

      i.   8   A-schools (officer or enlisted initial skills)
      ii. 52 C-Schools (enlisted Navy Enlisted Classification (NEC)-awarding schools)

      iii.   50 D-Schools (officer or enlisted professional development)

      iv.   76 F & T Schools (officer or enlisted Functional and Team training)

      v.   23 miscellaneous courses

f) Major examples of interoperable maritime skill-sets taught at these schools include:

      i.   Naval Aviation pilot training. In addition to pilot training, USCG reserves a US Naval Test Pilot School billet every 2 to 3 years to support critical USCG aviation developmental test programs.

      ii.   A Coast Guard Liaison Officer is assigned to the Center for Information Dominance Learning Site (CID LS) in Pensacola, FL. Additionally, there are two Coast Guard instructors teaching Navy courses at CID LS Pensacola. Other Coast Guard intelligence professionals routinely attend specific Navy training in support of Coast Guard Cryptologic operations.

      iii.   Explosive Ordnance Disposal

      iv.   Diving

      v.   Shipboard Damage Control and Firefighting

      vi.   Electronic Warfare

      vii.   Intelligence

      viii.   Water survival

      ix.   Tactical operations

      x.   Integrated Command System training for contingency responses

2) Fleet Training and Engagements:

a) The Navy's Fleet Response Training Plan (FRTP) provides opportunities for USN-USCG fleet training interactions from unit through staff level. Events include USCG liaison officers in pre-event planning conferences.

      i.   Opportunities through FY18 include USCG LNOs as a White Cell in Maritime Domain Awareness/Maritime Interception Operations (MDA/MIO) type scenarios in Fleet Synthetic Training (FST), and USCG cutters participating in Composite Unit Training Exercise (C2X)/Joint Task Force Exercise (JTFEX) MDA/MIO scenarios.

b) Counter Illicit Trafficking deployments and operations provide an excellent venue for USN-USCG interaction and refinement of interoperability.

      i.   In preparation for CIT deployments, USCG provides LNOs to assist USN aircrews by offering Airborne Use of Force (AUF) training, and a USCG Law Enforcement Detachment (LEDET) which embarks onboard USN surface ships to provide law enforcement training.

c) Navy and Coast Guard commanders (at both operational and support units) maintain mutually beneficial relationships that facilitate training, certification, and recertification requirements for both Services (e.g., USN aircraft working with Coast Guard deployable specialized forces to conduct refresher training on the rapid, at-sea delivery of forces). Locally-brokered training arrangements between commanders will continue to be encouraged by OPNAV and Coast Guard Headquarters staff.

d) Working groups, staff talks, and interoperability initiatives with USN/USCG and regional partner nations:

   i. Three Party Staff Talks (TPST): Conducted annually; developed to increase familiarity and formulate interoperability between three parties (East Coast: CG LANTAREA, USFF, and Maritime Forces Atlantic (MARLANT) – Royal Canadian Navy; West Coast: CG PACAREA, C3F, and Maritime Forces Pacific (MARPAC) - Royal Canadian Navy).

   ii. North American Maritime Security Initiative (NAMSI): NORTHCOM-directed initiative which includes USCG, USN, Royal Canadian Navy and Secretaría de Marina (SEMAR) - Armada de México. Conducted annually with exercises in both the Pacific and Gulf of Mexico.

   iii. Oceania Maritime Security Initiative (OMSI): C3F and C7F support USCG District 14 in the defense of Western/Central Pacific Island Exclusive Economic Zones against illegal fishing and illicit maritime activity.

   iv. Africa Maritime Law Enforcement Partnership (AMLEP): A major USN/USCG initiative in support of the Africa Partnership Station (APS), AMLEP is a series of activities designed to build maritime safety and security in Africa through working together with African and other international partners. Operations employ an African host nation's own law enforcement boarding team, along with a U.S. Coast Guard boarding team, operating from a U.S. Coast Guard or U.S. Navy vessel.

   v. Maritime Cryptologic Committee (MCC): The Coast Guard is a member of the Navy-initiated MCC developed to increase coordination and commonality among the cryptologic community.

e) Exercises:

   i. RIMPAC (Rim of the Pacific): Recurring biennial training exercises in the Pacific Fleet promoting regional maritime security with maritime partner nations will continue to include USCG participants.

ii. CARAT (Cooperation Afloat Readiness and Training): Annual USN exercise that includes a USCG Cutter and/or Law Enforcement Detachment personnel. Individual bilateral exercises with Brunei, Indonesia, Malaysia, Philippines, Singapore, Vietnam, Bangladesh, Cambodia, and Thailand.

iii. BALIKATAN: Annual PACOM Joint Field Training Exercise with the Philippine Armed Forces. USCG has provided LNOs for multilateral Humanitarian Assistance/Disaster Relief portion of a Table Top Exercise.

iv. FORTUNE GUARD Proliferation Security Initiative Exercise: New PACOM Joint Proliferation Security Initiative Exercise planned for August 2014. Envisioned to include a Table Top Exercise, Ashore Port Phase and an At-Sea Phase. USCG participation is to be determined. Location is planned to rotate among Australia, New Zealand, Japan, Singapore and Republic of Korea.

v. UNITAS: Combined South American and U.S.-sponsored annual exercise that includes a USCG Cutter and Law Enforcement Detachment personnel. It trains participating forces in a variety of maritime scenarios to test command and control of forces at sea, while operating as a multinational force to provide the maximum interoperability.

vi. VIGILANT SHIELD: NORAD-NORTHCOM scenario based exercise that focuses on Air/Maritime Warning/ Defense. The exercise provides a venue for COOP, Cyber (IO and IA), J-DIAMD, and other Commander's Priorities. USN and USCG play an active role in exercise planning and execution.

vii. ARDENT SENTRY: NORAD- NORTHCOM exercise designed to train the command headquarters and its components for their mission of providing defense support of civil authorities, on request. USN and USCG play an active role in exercise planning and execution.

viii. SOLID CURTAIN – CITADEL SHIELD: Test and improve MIDLANT region's Anti-Terrorism/Force Protection (AT/FP) readiness and reaction posture through simulating terrorist attacks on installations and commands. USCG supports local responses to waterborne threats to USN assets and installations.

ix. FRONTIER SENTINEL: USFF/ Coast Guard Atlantic Area/JTF-Atlantic (Canada)-sponsored exercise using live forces and headquarters staffs to evaluate interoperability and collaborative planning at the operational and tactical level of homeland defense and homeland security.

x. BOLD ALLIGATOR: Large scale amphibious event to exercise the Navy-Marine Corps' ability to conduct prompt and sustained amphibious expeditionary operations from the sea. USCG participates in port operations missions to include security, clearance and salvage.

3) Other Commonality Working Group(s) and Initiatives:

   a) USN/USCG Small Craft Commonality Integrated Process Team initiatives:

      i. Visit, Board, Search & Seizure Working Group: joint USCG/USN/USMC effort to identify potential training initiatives.
      ii. Special Missions Training Center: pipeline training for Level II (combat Coxswain). Integrated with USCG Core Training Strand.
      iii. Coastal Riverine Force (USN)/Port Security Unit (USCG): identify potential consolidation of training.

   b) Naval Logistics Integration Working Group initiatives:

      i. Identify opportunities to maximize efficiencies by combining training for like systems wherever practical (e.g., Common Logistics Solutions to Support Arctic Operations and LCS/NSC spares commonality).

   c) SSBN Transit Protection System Escort Steering Group (ESG)

      i. TPS Training Working Group is exploring USN/USCG opportunities for expanded use of the Transit Protection Training System (TPTS)

   d) DOD Inter-Agency Working Group sponsors the Integration and Exercise Workshop (IEW) in January 2014.

      i. Will highlight Combatant Commander, service, and interagency interaction.

   e) Update of U.S. Fleet Forces-COMLANTAREA Memorandum of Understanding (MOU) for training of USCG ships and personnel by Navy Afloat Training Groups (ATGs) is in development (expected completion, Q3 FY14).

   f) USCG LNOs are assigned to several USN Component Command and Numbered Fleet staffs to include: U.S. Fleet Forces Command; U.S. Pacific Fleet; U.S. 3rd Fleet; U.S. 7th Fleet; U.S. Naval Forces Southern Command/U.S. 4th Fleet; U.S. Naval Forces Central Command/U.S. 5th Fleet, and U.S. Naval Forces Europe-Africa/U.S. 6th Fleet. The Navy and Coast Guard also have over ninety personnel exchanged between services and assigned to ATGs and training centers. These personnel provide vital subject matter expertise and insight to their service counterparts.

c. FUTURE STATE (FY19 to FY23).

    1) Opportunities for commonality and interoperability:

      a) Continue Navy Fleet Synthetic Training and C2X/JTFEX training interactions to further refine training and capture emerging shared mission areas and tactics, techniques and procedures.

      b) Refine AUF and LEDET integration training to remain relevant against the evolving maritime threats.

    2) Recommended additional activities and initiatives:

      a) Promote partnerships, both within the U.S. Government and with international allies, in support of security and safety in the Arctic.

        i. Fleet training should leverage Operations and Exercises in the Arctic involving surface, aviation, and expeditionary units in concert with USCG units and USCG Arctic/near-Arctic operating sites.

        ii. Pursue additional agreements with Arctic nations to leverage capabilities and expand cooperative opportunities within the region.

        iii. Multinational Exercise Participation. Take advantage of opportunities to participate in Arctic regional exercises with USCG and regional/multinational partners.

      b) Institutionalize Naval Logistics Initiatives in Navy, Marine Corps and Coast Guard logistics training and education venues.

        i. Develop NLI expeditionary sustainment curriculum to produce Naval Service logisticians fully capable of supporting Naval Expeditionary Forces.

        ii. Examine Arctic operations lessons learned and incorporate into training and education.

5.4 COMMAND, CONTROL, AND COMMUNICATIONS (C3) SYSTEMS.

a. INTRODUCTION. The Permanent Joint Working Group (PJWG) has played an active role regarding C3 systems planning and coordination, and will likely continue to do so going forward. For example, in October 2012, the PJWG reviewed and discussed the proposed Navy Type-Navy Owned C3 suite for the Offshore Patrol Cutter, and forwarded a recommendation to senior Coast Guard and Navy leadership that was subsequently adopted. As the OPC program progresses from current state (FY14 to FY18) to future state (FY19 to FY23), the PJWG will continue to serve as a viable forum for both NTNO and Navy Type Coast Guard Owned (NTCGO) C3 systems dialogue between the Navy and Coast Guard. The same holds true for other acquisition programs (e.g., Fast Response Cutter and National Security Cutter), as well as legacy fleet platforms.

b. CURRENT STATE (FY14 to FY18).

1) Coast Guard COMDTINST 7100.2G, Support of Navy Type-Navy Owned Combat Systems, provides guidance on how Navy funding is distributed to support all NTNO systems in Coast Guard custody. Program management and support of legacy systems to meet Naval Operational Capabilities (NOC) requirement resides in the Office of Navy Combat Systems, CG-6432.

2) The Coast Guard utilizes the following Navy Program of Record Cryptologic Afloat Communications systems onboard NSCs: Automated Digital Network System (ADNS), Sensitive Compartmented Information (SCI) Networks, and Extremely High Frequency (EHF) Satellite Communications (SATCOM). The Coast Guard utilizes SCI Networks onboard 270-foot Medium Endurance Cutters (WMECs).

3) The recommended NTCGO systems to meet C3 commonality and interoperability for future NSCs and OPCs are ADNS, Consolidated Afloat Network Enterprise Services (CANES) and Navy Multiband Terminal (NMT).

4) The recommended NTNO systems to meet C3 commonality and interoperability for the OPC are as follows: MIL UHF LOS 225-400 MHZ (Digital Modular Radio (DMR), ARC-210, PRC-117); MIL UHF SATCOM (DMR, ARC-210, PRC-117); Messaging (DMR SATCOM, ARC-210, PRC-117); LINK 11; Joint Range Extension (JRE) Link-16, forwarded LINK 22; VACM (KY-100M, KY-58M, KYV-5M).

5) Coast Guard will utilize Navy Program of Record for Mobile User Objective System (MUOS). An example includes the DMR on POLAR Class Cutters.

6) National Security Cutter was designed with interoperability in mind and has Common Data Link Management System (CDLMS), Global Command and Control System (GCCS), Aegis Baseline 9 (Tactical Domain), and Navigation Sensor System Interface (NAVSSI) as Navy Type-Coast Guard Owned (NTCGO). The Services shall work together to establish appropriate NSC NTCGO items as NTNO via a similar process for the OPC.

7) Coast Guard Acquisitions CG-9322, CG-9335, and CG-761 have been working with Program Executive Office (PEO) Command, Control, Communications, Computers, and Intelligence (C4I) – Priority Material Office (PMW) 760 and Integrated Warfare System (IWS) 1.0 as well as NAVAIR to identify technical interfaces for each Command, Control, Communications, Computers, Intelligence, Surveillance, and

Reconnaissance (C4ISR) and Combat Weapon System to ensure compatibility with the OPC.

8) Mobile User Objective System End to End (E2E) Operational Integration Working Group (OIWG).

USCG Surface Assets with USN Commonality

General System Name	Boats	In-Service Cutter Classes	Fast Response Cutter	National Security Cutter	Offshore Patrol Cutter
Communications					
High Frequency (HF), Very High Frequency (VHF) & Ultra High Frequency (UHF) Communication Systems	X	X	X	X	X
Military Satellite Communications (MILSATCOM)		X	X	X	X
Extremely High Frequency (EHF)				X	
Naval Modular Automated Communications System (NAVMACS)		X		X	X
Integrated Voice Communication System (IVCS)			X	X	
Radars					
Multi-Mode Radars				X	X
Air Search Radar (TRS3D, SPS-40, etc.)		X		X	
Fire Control (SPQ-9B, MK 92)		X		X	
Command Control					
Identification Friend or Foe (IFF)		X	X	X	X
GPS Systems		X		X	X
Wind/Metrological Systems		X		X	X
AEGIS Libraries				X	
C4ISR Data Collection and Analysis		X		X	
Encryption					
Type I Encryption devices (KG-84, KIV-7, TACLANE, etc.)		X	X	X	X
Tactical Systems					
Tactical Data Link Systems (Link 11)		(378 only)		X	X
Electronic Warfare Systems (SLQ-32, SEWIP, WLR-1, etc.)		X		X	X
Decoy Launching System		X		X	X

(continued)

General System Name	Boats	In-Service Cutter Classes	Fast Response Cutter	National Security Cutter	Offshore Patrol Cutter
Ships Signal Exploitation Equipment System				X	
Networks					
Sensitive Compartmented Information Networks		X		X	X
Network Routing (Advanced Digital Networking System)				X	
Aviation C4ISR					
Unmanned Aircraft System (UAS)				X	X
Tactical Air Navigation (TACAN)		X	X	X	X
Certifications					
Software System Safety Technical Review Board (SSSTRP)				X	X
Training					
System/Component Training (provided by Navy)		X		X	X

c. FUTURE STATE (FY19 to FY23). Revolves around maintaining previously established efforts and exploring new areas to further assist in financial reductions while remaining mission capable.

5.5 SENSORS.

a. INTRODUCTION. The current and future inventory of Fleet systems is rich with sensor systems, and as a result the PJWG has played, and will continue to play, an active role advocating for sensor commonality and interoperability in support of Naval Warfare mission readiness. From fire control radars and electronic warfare systems to electro-optical sights integrated into gun weapons systems, the Navy and Coast Guard will continue to pursue common sensor systems, and the PJWG will continue to play a governance role.

b. CURRENT STATE (FY14 to FY18).

1) Coast Guard COMDTINST 7100.2G, Support of Navy Type-Navy Owned Combat Systems, provides guidance on how Navy funding is distributed in support of all Navy Type-Navy Owned systems in Coast Guard custody. Program management and support of legacy systems to help meet NOC requirements resides in the Office of Navy Combat Systems, CG-6432.

2) The recommended NTNO systems to meet Sensor commonality and interoperability for the Offshore Patrol Cutter are as follows: TACAN; Multi-Mode Radar; IFF; SEWIP (SLQ-32/SSX-1 replacement); and MK-160, Gun System.

3) National Security Cutter was designed to have common sensors with the Navy, specifically: TRS-3D; MK-160; SLQ-32; Ship's Signals Exploitation Equipment (SSEE); Cryptologic Carry-On Program (CCOP); TACAN; and IFF.

4) Coast Guard Acquisitions CG-9322, CG-9335, and CG-761 have been working with PEO C4I – PMW 760 and IWS 1.0 to identify technical interfaces for each C4ISR and Combat Weapon System to ensure compatibility with the OPC.

5) Coast Guard Maritime Intelligence Fusion Centers are integral partners with the Naval Research Laboratory, Office of Naval Intelligence, and Fleet Forces Command in the Joint development of global vessel identification and tracking services now in use throughout the Fleet.

c. FUTURE STATE (FY19 to FY23).

1) Discuss future Electronic and Cryptologic Support equipment, including CCOP, SSEE, and Integrated Broadcast Service/Common Interactive Broadcast services.

2) Revolves around maintaining previously established efforts and exploring new areas to further assist in financial reductions while remaining mission capable.

3) Discuss opportunities to enhance enterprise-level vessel identification and tracking services through the fusion of data from systems such as the Nationwide Automatic Identification System, the Long Range Identification and Tracking program, and the Air and Maritime Operations Surveillance System.

5.6 WEAPON SYSTEMS.

a. INTRODUCTION. Weapons systems serve as the tactical means for USN and USCG defense and protection. With strategic investments by both departments, each service leveraged cost savings and increased capability in their joint efforts. In the Weapons domain, Coast Guard Commandant Instruction (COMDTINST) 7100.2G, Support of Navy Type-Navy Owned Combat Systems, provides guidance on how Navy funding is distributed to support all NTNO systems in the USCG. Leveraging the NTNO relationship augments the commonality and efficiencies achieved through the utilization of standard systems, training, and certifications. Since the initiation of the National Fleet Policy, much progress has been made. The following table summarizes major areas allowing for interagency agreements, integrated product teams, and coalitions to allow for commonality and efficiencies in fiscally constraining times.

b. CURRENT STATE (FY14 to FY18).

USCG Surface Assets with USN Commonality

General System Name	Boats	In-Service Cutter Classes	Fast Response Cutter	National Security Cutter	Offshore Patrol Cutter
Weapons					
Close In Weapons System (CIWS)		X		X	
Machine Gun System (25mm)		X	X		X
Gun Weapon System (76mm, 57mm)		X		X	X
Machine Gun System (.50 Caliber)		X	X	X	X
M16A2 / M4A2	X	X	X	X	X
AN/SLQ-32, SEWIP, and AN/SSQ-137 (Inc. E) Electronic Attack systems				X	X
Decoy Launching System MK-53				X	X
Training					
Battle Force Electronic Warfare Trainer (BEWT)		X		X	X
57mm/76mm Training		X		X	X
System/Component Training (provided by Navy)		X		X	X
Certifications					
Weapons System Explosives Safety Review Board (WSESRB)				X	X

c. FUTURE STATE (FY19 to FY23). The future state for commonality in the Weapons domain revolves around maintaining previously established efforts and exploring new areas to further assist in financial reductions while remaining mission capable. The following list outlines additional areas for exploration of interagency commonality.

1) Stabilized small arms mounts.
2) Maintenance and sparing of weapon systems.
3) Joint weapons certification.
4) Weapon systems training courses for equipment.

5.7 ENGINEERING SYSTEMS.

a. INTRODUCTION. Commonality and interoperability for Engineering Systems of the U.S. Coast Guard and Navy produced increased operational effectiveness and cost savings for both military organizations. Joint efforts positively influenced platform design, equipment selection, weapon system sustainability and maintenance support services/methodologies. The significance of this collaboration promoted cost efficiencies within the following focus areas:

1) Acquisition process and requirements development.
2) Configuration management.
3) Research and development.
4) Operation and maintenance asset Life Cycle Cost.

b. CURRENT STATE (FY14 to FY18).

1) A USCG/NAVSEA Memorandum of Agreement (MOA) establishes a NAVSEA Lead Systems Engineer to coordinate engineering support provided to the USCG. This single point of contact manages engineering services provided by NAVSEA which includes Hull, Mechanical, Electrical, Combat Systems Design, Cost Engineering, Industrial Analysis, C4I and Aviation issues that have shipboard integration implications.

   a) The USCG has funded over 200 Military Interdepartmental Purchase Requests (MIPRs) to NAVSEA since the establishment of this MOA in 2008.
   b) The MOA allows the USCG access to NAVSEA Warfare Centers encompassing Engineering and fleet support centers for offensive and defensive systems associated with surface warfare as well as homeland and national defense systems from the sea.

2) OPNAV Instruction 4000.79B (Policy For U.S. Navy Provision and Support of Specified Equipment and Systems to the U.S. Coast Guard) documents the Navy policy to ensure that the Coast Guard is prepared to carry out assigned naval warfare tasks mutually agreed upon by the two services.

   a) This instruction establishes the plan, program and budget within overall Navy priorities, for specified navy military equipment, systems and logistics support requirements for Coast Guard units to ensure that the Coast Guard is prepared to execute naval warfare tasks in concert with U.S. Navy units. NAVSEA Program Executive Office, Integrated Warfare Systems has established a MOA with the USCG for the procurement and life cycle support of NTNO Weapon and Sensor Systems for USCG Surface Platforms.
   b) The USCG provides NTNO Ordnance Program Management by applying and enforcing all USCG policy applicable to the repair and maintenance of all NTNO Systems used by the USCG to ensure continued compliance with the Basic Inter-service Agreement, supporting the combat weapons systems outlined by the NAVSEA PEO IWS/USCG MOA and OPNAVINST 4000.79B.

3) Two high level MOA/Inter-agency Agreements exist between USCG and NAVAIR's Naval Air Warfare Division and Naval Aviation PEOs. These provide for NAVAIR support across the spectrum of manned and unmanned aircraft/system acquisition, modification, test, analysis and airworthiness certification support and cutter-based aviation capabilities certification. Additional MOAs perform the following:

    a) Establish NAVAIR as the USCG aviation Certified TEMPEST Technical Authority

    b) Establish NAVAIR PMA-209 as the Lead Integrator for the HC-130H A1U Upgrade Program

    c) Establish a cooperative agreement between CG-711 and PEO (U&W) PMA-266 for MQ-8 Fire Scout cooperation

c. FUTURE STATE (FY19 to FY23).

1) Improve active agreements between NAVSEA and the Coast Guard to expand and leverage research and development efforts applicable to advancing science and technology.

2) Further the utilization of web based integrated digital/data environments, such as the Naval Systems Engineering Resource Center, to provide focused standardization of systems engineering and technical authority policy, processes, tools, standards and architectures across the Navy and Coast Guard.

3) Increase service collaboration in the selection and evaluation of mature commercial technologies that meet naval & aviation engineering system application and functionality.

5.8 PLATFORMS.

a. INTRODUCTION. Large platform assets serve as the keystone of all Naval and Maritime activities and allow us to perform our missions. The Platform domain is the most critical to the USN and USCG for mission execution. With strategic investments by both departments, each service leverages cost savings and increased capability in their joint efforts. In the Platform domain, commonality and efficiencies are achieved with the utilization of standard requirements, systems, management, equipment, logistics, and certifications. Since the initiation of the National Fleet Policy, much progress has been accomplished. The following tables summarize major areas for surface and aviation platforms to pursue interagency agreements, integrated product teams, and coalitions to allow for commonality and efficiencies in fiscally constraining times.

b. CURRENT STATE (FY14 to FY18).

USCG Surface Assets with USN Commonality

General System Name	Boats	In-Service Cutter Classes	Fast Response Cutter	National Security Cutter	Offshore Patrol Cutter
Standards					
Steel Vessel Rules				X	
Naval Vessel Rules			X		X
Institute of Electrical and Electronics Engineers (IEEE) Industry Standards	X	X	X	X	X
American Bureau of Shipping (ABS) Standards		X	X	X	X
Systems					
Navigation System (NAVSSI)				X	
Machinery Control Systems (MCS)		X	X	X	X
Damage Control Software		X		X	X
Bridge Mounted Multi-Function RADIAC (BMMFR)				X	X
Improved Point Detection System				X	X
Flight Deck Lighting		X		X	X
Wind Indicating System		X		X	X
TACAN		X		X	X
IFF		X	X	X	X
Management					
SUPSHIP Production Manpower				X	
Shipbuilding Rates Adjudication				X	
Defense Contract Audit Agency (DCAA) Audit Services				X	
Equipment					
Life Rafts		X	X	X	X
Self-Contained Breathing Apparatus (SCBA)		X	X	X	X
Stabilized Glide Slope Indicating Systems		X		X	X
Wave Off Light System		X		X	X
Logistics					
Engineering Operational Sequencing System (EOSS) / Combat Systems Operational Sequencing System (CSOSS)			X	X	X
Training					
LM 2500 marine gas turbine engine				X	

(continued)

General System Name	Boats	In-Service Cutter Classes	Fast Response Cutter	National Security Cutter	Offshore Patrol Cutter
System/Component Training (provided by Navy)		X		X	X
Certifications & Analysis					
Topside Analysis		X		X	X
Commander Operational Test & Evaluation Force (COMOPTEVFOR) serves as Operational Test Authority (OTA)			X	X	X
Board of Inspection and Survey (INSURV) Vessel Acceptance				X	X
Combat Ship Systems Qualification Trials (CSSQT)				X	X
Degaussing		X		X	
NAVAIR Aviation Facility Certification for all air-capable Cutters (includes legacy cutters)		X		X	X

USCG Aviation Assets with USN Commonality

General System Name	HC-130J	HC-130H	HC-144	MH-60	MH-65	C-37	UAS
Standards							
NAVAIR Airworthiness standards for airworthiness recommendation	X	X	X	X			X
Systems							
IFF	X	X	X	X	X		
TACAN	X	X	X	X	X		
Talos Mission Processing System (EP-3 Minotaur variant with OSI)	X		X				
USN H-60F airframes for USCG MH-60T Conversions				X			
Management							
Defense Contract Audit Agency (DCAA) Audit Services	X						
Equipment							
Sundowned USN SH-60Fs – PMA-299				X			
Fire Scout TCDL, GCS, UCARS – PMA-266							X
Logistics							
HC-130J PBL Support – PMA-207	X						
Training							
Maintenance training support				X	X		

(continued)

General System Name	HC-130J	HC-130H	HC-144	MH-60	MH-65	C-37	UAS
Certifications & Analysis							
NAVAIR Aviation Communications, Navigation Surveillance/Air Traffic Management (CNS/ATM) Certification standards for certification recommendation		X		X			
NAVAIR IFF/AIMS Certification support		X	X	X			
NAVAIR TEMPEST/COMSEC Certification testing standards	X	X	X	X	X	X	
NAVAIR Test, evaluation, analysis support to all USCG aviation assets	X	X	X	X	X	X	X

Small platform asset commonality has greatly assisted both the Navy and Coast Guard. Navy purchased Response Boat – Mediums (RB-Ms) and Response Boat - Smalls (RB-Ss) for port security and force protection. Current Coast Guard small boat acquisition contracts allow for options exercising further Navy acquisition of these platforms. The following table establishes current state for small craft.

USCG Small Craft with USN Commonality

General System Name	Boats
Acquisitions	
Joint Procurements	X
Joint Requirements/Specification Development	X
Training	
Level II Combat COXN Training	X
Logistics	
Consolidated Training, Equipment and Mission Execution	X

   c. FUTURE STATE. The future state for commonality in the Platform domain revolves around maintaining previously established efforts and exploring new areas to further assist in financial reductions while remaining mission capable. The following list establishes new areas for exploration of interagency commonality, while maintaining the current state.

     1) Propulsion systems and components.
     2) Unmanned aircraft systems.
     3) Aviation sensor integration.

4) Joint weapons certification.
5) Stern launch and recovery training.
6) System and mission readiness training courses.

6. <u>PROGRAMMATIC COLLABORATION</u>. As The Federal Government's discretionary budget is projected to decrease over the next several years, the Navy and the Coast Guard must seek economies and synergies to further reduce spending. Accordingly, during this period of budgetary uncertainty, it is critical that both services remain good stewards of the Nation's resources by closely cooperating to develop more interoperable and affordable forces.

As resources permit, the Navy and Coast Guard will cooperate to achieve complementary, non-redundant capability and capacity in areas outlined by Sections 5.1 through 5.8. Such interoperability will enable both Services to support each other's mission sets such as Undersea Warfare (USW), Expeditionary Warfare, Strike Warfare, Strategic Sealift, Marine Force Protection Units, Regional Security Cooperation, Humanitarian Assistance/ Disaster Relief (HA/DR), Defense Support of Civil Authorities (DSCA), Counter-Illicit Trafficking, Counter-Piracy, Maritime Interception Operations, Theater Security Cooperation, and Visit, Board, Search, and Seizure Missions around the world; to promote the safe, secure, efficient and free flow of global commerce; to operate effectively in all potential climatic conditions; and to meet emerging requirements in the Arctic maritime region.

The initiatives listed in the Fleet Plan, when properly implemented, will increase commonality and interoperability between the Navy and Coast Guard. They will positively impact the resource/programming efforts of both services by avoiding redundancies, achieving economies of scale, improving operational effectiveness and providing a mechanism to enhance integration and resource development.

7. <u>INTEGRATED PLAN OF ACTION AND MILESTONES</u>.

a. Current and Evolving Operations.

1) FY14, Q3: Charter a joint USN/USCG Arctic Working Group. Create a formal partnership between the Navy and Coast Guard to examine synergistic missions, requirements, and capabilities in the unique Arctic operating environment. This group will utilize a collaborative approach to support the *U.S. National Strategy for the Arctic Region* in order to ensure a stable and secure region where U.S. national interests are safeguarded and the homeland is protected.
Lead: N51, CG-DCO-X

2) FY14 to FY18: Navy will gradually assume responsibility for domestic Force Protection for non-TPS HVU escorts in Fleet Concentration Areas. Coast Guard will focus on domestic non-TPS HVU escort efforts outside of those areas. Both Services will leverage existing assets to maintain a risk-informed, non-TPS HVU protection mission and refine processes to improve information sharing, scheduling, and operational planning in all locations. Best practices from proven units will be

incorporated to shape future guidelines based on mission risk and prioritization. Coast Guard will continue to provide TPS escorts in accordance with the 2006 TPS MOA. The TPS escort force package is made feasible through the authorized reimbursable agreement in the Economy Act and through extensive USN/USCG collaboration.
Lead: N31, SSP, CG-MSR, CG-741

3) FY14 to FY15: Continue to refine requirements and capabilities for adaptive force package options. Standardize terms of reference and operational guidelines.
Lead: USFF, CG-ODO, CG-MLE

4) FY14 to FY18: Annually review Terms of Reference (TOR)/MOA/MOU to validate joint processes and personnel exchanges between services. Recommend additional TOR/MOA/MOUs to address initiatives as appropriate.
Lead: Fleet Board

   a) FY14: Draft MOA for Coast Guard Liaison Officer in N96 Surface Warfare.
   Lead: N96, CG-7

5) FY14 to FY18: Continue to pursue opportunities to base USCG units on USN installations in order to identify potential economies of scale and maximize use of existing infrastructure. Leverage shared homeporting to capitalize on opportunities for joint training and temporary personnel exchanges.
Lead: N51, CG-7

6) FY14 to FY18: Advance national efforts to improve MDA through expanded collaboration by advocating participation in the Maritime Safety & Security Information System (MSSIS) or follow-on system; pursuing standards-based data exchanges to share maritime data in keeping with the National MDA Architecture; ensuring data from available sensors are made available to existing enterprise services/solutions; and introducing common lexicon for MDA leveraging existing Vessel of Interest (VOI) lexicon.
Lead: N2N6, CG-2

b. Integrated Logistics.

1) (FY14 to FY18)

   a) Continue established NLI Governance.
   Lead: N41, CG-4
   b) Continue LCS/NSC parts commonality identification.
   Lead: N41, CG-4 Support: NAVSUP
   c) Identify commonality opportunities between OPC, LCS and NSC.
   Lead: N41, CG-4
   d) Coordinate Corrosion Control best practices and resources across Services.
   Lead: N41, CG-4 Support: NAVSEA, NAVAIR

e) Investigate common logistics for dive support.
   Lead: N41, CG-4 Support: NAVSEA

f) Conduct additional analysis of best practices and procedures for cases where the Navy stops supporting a legacy system and transfers full responsibility to the Coast Guard. (i.e. MK 92 Radar)
   Lead: N96, CG-4 Support: NAVSEA

g) Establish continual demand/Stock on Hand data sharing capabilities for LCS/NSC.
   Lead: N41, CG-4 Support: NAVSUP

h) Leverage contracting efficiencies. Develop common support contracts for LCS/NSC.
   Lead: N41, CG-4 Support: NAVSUP

i) Identify additional facility and infrastructure efficiency opportunities. (Ex. Transit Protection support facilities, training sites, local maintenance support)
   Lead: N46, CG-4

j) Increase cooperation and reduce costs of environmental assessments and impact statements.
   Lead: N45, CG-4

2) (FY19 to FY23)

a) Continue established NLI Governance.
   Lead: N41, CG-4

b) Establish common maintenance contracts for LCS/NSC/OPC.
   Lead: N41, CG-4 Support: N41

c) Identify future technologies. (e.g., additive manufacturing)
   Lead: N41, CG-4 Support: NAVSUP

d) Continue current NLI Integrated Product Teams (IPT) and create new teams to achieve future identified efforts as required.
   Lead: N41, CG-4

e) Explore joint Research and Development efforts for future capabilities and cost efficiencies.
   Lead: N41, CG-4 Support: ONR

f) Investigate cross-service targeted allowancing of LCS/NSC/OPC repair parts.
   Lead: N41, CG-4 Support: NAVSUP

g) Develop potential methods and business rules to reduce part redundancy through sharing a single inventory of common items.
   Lead: N41, CG-4 Support: NAVSUP

h) Investigate methods to integrate or enable sharing of data between Navy and CG logistics business/IT Systems.
   Lead: N41, CG-4

i) Increase cooperation and reduce costs of environmental assessments and impact statements.
   Lead: N45, CG-4

c. Training.

  1) FY14 to FY18: Continue USN/USCG training interaction efforts to include planning conferences, exercises, and participation in synthetic and at-sea training events.
  Lead: USFF/CPF, FORCECOM

    a) Increase USCG participation in joint integrated training and Fleet Response Training Plan events to better prepare for forward deployed Phase 0 and combat operations.

    b) Under a resource-constrained environment, increase cooperation in blending operations to meet USN training and certification while simultaneously meeting USCG MLE requirements, across the spectrum of USN capabilities and assets.

  2) FY14 to FY23: Identify and develop feedback mechanisms to determine effectiveness of training between USCG and USN. Examine opportunities for potential efficiencies by consolidating USCG and USN training.

    a) Individual/Specialized Skills Training.
        Lead: NETC, FORCECOM

    b) Fleet/Operational Training and Engagement.
        Lead: USFF/CPF, FORCECOM

  3) FY14 to FY18: Leverage IEW series of workshops to continue to socialize and identify emerging USN-USCG opportunities for beneficial training interactions.
  Lead: USFF/CPF, FORCECOM

  4) FY14 to FY23: Draft and approve new training related MOU(s) and periodically revisit existing MOUs to ensure currency and relevancy (annually at a minimum).

    a) Individual/Specialized Skill Training MOUs/MOAs (e.g., Inter-Service Training Review Organization).
        Lead: NETC/BUPERS-00C2, FORCECOM

    b) Fleet/Operational Training and Engagement MOUs/MOAs (e.g., USFF-COMLANTAREA).
        Lead: USFF/CPF, FORCECOM

  5) FY14 to FY23: USN training stakeholders monitor developments from emerging DOD Arctic strategy, policy and operations plans to ensure USCG is included in relevant Arctic-related training events.
  Lead: USFF/CPF, FORCECOM

a) Leverage and coordinate USFF/C3F training events, presence operations, capabilities, and support to USCG management of the Arctic and International Straits.

d. C3 Systems.

1) FY14 to FY23: Navy and Coast Guard will continue to follow policy set forth in the following instructions when evaluating systems for Navy and Coast Guard use:

   a) Policy for U.S. Navy Provisions and Support of Specified Equipment and Systems to the U.S. Coast Guard, OPNAVINST 4000.79B.
   b) U.S. Navy – U.S. Coast Guard Communications Policy, OPNAVINST 2000.20D/ COMDTINST 2009.
   c) OPNAVINST F2300.44H Command, Control, Communications and Computer Requirements for Navy Ships, Military Sealift Command Ships, Coast Guard Cutters, Transportable Facilities, Designated Craft, Portable Radio Users, Major Shore Communication Stations, and Maritime Operations Centers.

2) FY14: PEO C4I is developing Road Maps for USCG C4I NTNO systems to match the Navy's modernization plan.
   Lead: N2/N6F, N96, CG-761

3) FY14: Develop cross military funding strategy to ensure critical NTCGO systems can receive changes from Navy when required.
   Lead: N2/N6F, N96, CG-761

4) FY14: Start dialogue with OPNAV regarding unifying NSC's NTCGO C3 Systems equipment into NTNO program.
   Lead: N2/N6F, N96, CG-761

e. Sensors.

1) FY14 to FY23: Navy and Coast Guard will continue to follow policy set forth in the following instructions when evaluating systems for Navy and Coast Guard use:

   a) Policy for U.S. Navy Provisions and Support of Specified Equipment and Systems to the U.S. Coast Guard, OPNAVINST 4000.79B.
   b) U.S. Navy – U.S. Coast Guard Communications Policy, OPNAVINST 2000.20D/ COMDTINST 2009.
   c) OPNAVINST F2300.44H Command, Control, Communications and Computer Requirements for Navy Ships, Military Sealift Command Ships, Coast Guard Cutters, Transportable Facilities, Designated Craft, Portable Radio Users, Major Shore Communication Stations, and Maritime Operations Centers.

2) FY14: PEO C4I is developing Road Maps for USCG C4I NTNO systems to match the Navy's modernization plan.
Lead: N2/N6F, N96, CG-761

3) FY14: Develop cross military funding strategy to ensure critical NTCGO systems can receive changes from Navy when required.
Lead: N2/N6F, N96, CG-761

4) FY14: Start dialogue between OPNAV and CGHQ regarding unifying NSC's NTCGO Sensor equipment into NTNO program.
Lead: N2/N6F, N96, CG-761 Support: NAVSEA, CG-751

f. Weapon Systems.

1) FY14 to FY23: Continue to maximize commonality initiatives to enhance capabilities, reduce cost, and foster naval warfare readiness. It is our goal to continue established efforts while seeking additional efforts to allow both departments to be efficient in the Naval/Maritime Domain. As we progress, both departments will go through the below tasks to ensure adherence to the Fleet Commonality Policy:

   a) Continue to work with Program Acquisition Resource Managers (PARMs).
   Lead: N96, CG-751 Support: N98, NAVSEA, CG-721, CG-761
   b) Identify future technology refreshes.
   Lead: N96, CG-751 Support: N98, NAVSEA, CG-721, CG-761
   c) Align with interagency requirements for future systems.
   Lead: N96, CG-751 Support: N2/N6F, N98, NAVSEA, CG-721, CG-761
   d) Continue Integrated Product Team (IPT) and Joint Working Group participation.
   Lead: N96, CG-751
   e) Create new IPTs to achieve future efforts.
   Lead: N96, CG-751
   f) Continue Inter Agency Agreements between Warfare Centers and Program Offices.
   Lead: N96, CG-751
   g) Explore joint Research & Development efforts to identify future capabilities and cost efficiencies.
   Lead: N96, CG-751 Support: N98, NAVSEA, CG-721, CG-761

g. Engineering Systems.

1) R & D:
   a) FY14 to FY18: Fuel Cells. Collaborate on studies involving fuel cells/alternate power.
   Lead: N96, CG-45 Support: NAVSEA

2) Concept Design/Technical Authority/Modernization:
   a) FY14 to FY18: Establish a consistent, repeatable design processes for developing concept designs for the USCG.
      Lead: N96, CG-45 Support: NAVSEA
   b) FY14: Establish a USCG Concept Design Technical Warrant Holder Program to ensure consistent development of quality Concept Designs.
      Lead: N96, CG-45 Support: NAVSEA
   c) FY14 to FY18: Standardize shipyard production and reporting practices between USCG and USN projects in the same depot repair facility.
      Lead: N96, CG-45

d. Platforms.

1) FY14 to FY23: Continue to maximize commonality initiatives to enhance capabilities, reduce cost, and allow for mission execution. It is our goal to continue established efforts while seeking to allow both departments to be more efficient in the Naval/Maritime Domain. As we progress, both departments will go through the below tasks to ensure adherence to the Fleet Commonality Policy:

   a) Continue to work with Program Offices, Warfare Centers, and Support Facilities.
      Lead: N96, CG-751, CG-761, CG-721 Support: N95, NAVSEA, NAVAIR, CNIC
   b) Identify future technologies.
      Lead: N96, CG-751, CG-761, CG-721 Support: N95, SPAWAR, NSWCs, NAVSEA, NAVAIR
   c) Align with interagency requirements and standards for future systems and shipbuilding.
      Lead: N96, CG-751 Support: NAVSEA, NAVAIR
   d) Continue IPT and Joint Working Group participation.
      Lead: N96, CG-751 Support: N95, N98, N2/N6F, NAVSEA, NAVAIR, CG-721, CG-761
   e) Create new IPTs as needed to achieve future efforts.
      Lead: N96, CG-751
   f) Continue Inter Agency Agreements between Warfare Centers and Program Offices. Lead: N96, CG-751 Support: N95, NAVSEA, NAVAIR
   g) Explore joint Research & Development efforts as required to identify future capabilities and cost efficiencies.
      Lead: N96, CG-751 Support: N95, ONR, NSWCs

8. NAVY-COAST GUARD MEMORANDA OF UNDERSTANDING/AGREEMENT.

Memoranda of Understanding

Description	Type	Parties	Date
Advanced Marine Technology Development	MOU	N96, CG-7	19 Jun 81
Establish a Mine Countermeasures Mission for the Coast Guard	MOU	VCNO, VCG	19 May 82
Commonality Between LCS and NSC/WMEC/WPB	MOU	PEO Surface Strike, PEO Integrated Deepwater System	12 Apr 02
Establish NAVAIR as the USCG aviation Certified TEMPEST Technical Authority	MOU	NAWCAD, CG-41 (ALC)	30 Apr 03
Joint Harbor Operations Centers	MOU	VCNO, VCG	29 Aug 05
Establishes Intent by the USCG to use the Board of Inspection and Survey to Assist with the Conduct of Trials on Surface Assets, and the Intent of the Board to Provide Support	MOU	USN (INSURV), G-DPM-4	26 Sep 03
Force Advanced Warfare Concept Technology Program	MOU	USN, CG-711	21 May 09
US Navy Helicopter Support to Airborne Use of Force in Counter Drug Operations	MOU	USN, USCG	10 Aug 11
Establish PMA-209 as the Lead Integrator for the HC-130H A1U Upgrade Program	MOU	NAVAIR AIR-1.0, CG-93	08 Aug 12

Memoranda of Agreement

Description	Type	Parties	Date
Responsibility for Operating and Manning the Five US Navy Icebreakers	MOA	USN, USCG	22 Jul 65
Cooperation in Oil Spill Clean-up Operations and Salvage Operations	MOA	N4, USCG	15 Sep 80

Description	Type	Parties	Date
Designation of Coast Guard Area Commanders as Maritime Defense Zone Commanders	MOA	CNO, CCG	07 Mar 84
Mine Warfare Environmental Surveys of U.S. Ports	MOA	N2/N6E, USCG	22 Jul 86
Naval Ordnance Center Inventory Management and Systems Division	MOA	Naval Ordnance Center, USCG (CG-751)	13 Jan 97
Describes the Execution of Security Assistance Program	MOA	Navy IPO, CG-DCO-I	26 Mar 04
Describes USCG Procurement of Navy Type, Navy Owned Weapons and Sensors	MOA	NAVIWS, CG-D	04 Apr 04
Describes USCG Use of NAVSEA Supervisor of Shipbuilding, Conversion and Repair, Gulf Coast	MOA	NAVSEA, CG-DPM	19 Apr 04
Fleet Ballistic Submarine In-Transit Escort	MOA	VCNO, VCG	16 Aug 06
Life Cycle Support of Navy Type, Navy Owned Weapons and Sensor Systems	MOA	PEO Integrated Warfare Systems, PEO Integrated Deepwater Systems	07 Feb 07
Establishes a NAVSEA Lead Systems Engineer to Coordinate Engineering Support Provided to USCG	MOA	NAVSEA (SEA 05), CG-4, CG-9	25 Feb 08
Cooperative Agreement for MQ-8 Fire Scout Cooperation	MOA	NAVAIR PMA-266, CG-711	06 Oct 08
Describes USCG Obtaining Technical and Other Support Services from SPAWARSYSCEN Atlantic	MOA	SPAWARCEN Atlantic, USCG	19 May 09
Facilitates Collaborative Research and Development of Interest Between the USCG and NAVSEA	MOA	NAVSEA (SEA05WTD), CG-711	21 May 09
Establishes the Working Relationship Between the USCG (CG-922) and FISC Puget Sound to Provide Transportation Support via the DTS for USCG FMS Projects	MOA	FISC Puget Sound, CG-922	06 Jul 09

Description	Type	Parties	Date
Naval Sea Systems Command Warfare Centers	MOA	USN, USCG	08 Jul 09
NAWCAD Support Across the Spectrum of Manned and Unmanned Aircraft/System Acquisition, Airworthiness Certification Support, and Cutter-Based Aviation Capabilities	MOA	NAWCAD, CG-91	18 Sep 09
Naval Aviation PEO NAVAIR Support Across the Spectrum of Manned and Unmanned Aircraft/System Acquisition	MOA	PEO(A), PEO(T), PEO(U&W), AIR-1.0. CG-91	22 Dec 09
Defines the Basis by Which the USCG RDC May Obtain Technical and Other Support Services from the NRL for Research and Development	MOA	NRL, USCG RDC	18 Mar 10
Conduct of Independent Operational Test and Evaluation for Designated CG Acquisitions	MOA	COMOPTEVFOR, CG-7, CG-9	26 Jul 10
Exchange of Dive Personnel Billets and Mutual Dive Program Support	MOA	USN, CG-721	03 Feb 11
Support of Ships Signals Exploitation Equipment, Carry On Program, Networks and Communications Systems	MOA	N2/N6, VCG	14 Feb 11
Coast Guard Liaison to OPNAV N3/N5	MOA	N3/N5, DCO	15 Mar 11
Sector Command Center – Joint Program	MOA	USN, USCG (CG-741)	09 Sep 11
USCG Requests for Long Term Stationing of Assets at USN Installations	MOA	N3/N5, DCO	21 Mar 12
USN/USCG Joint Craft/Boat Capabilities and Acquisitions	MOA	N85, CG-7, CG-9	02 Apr 12

9. LEGAL AUTHORITIES.

U.S. Code Section	Short Title	Summary
10 USC § 101	Definitions	Defines "armed forces" to include the Coast Guard.
10 USC § 124	Detection & monitoring of aerial & maritime transit of illegal drugs	DoD is the lead agency for detection and monitoring of aerial & maritime transit of illegal drugs in support of law enforcement including USCG
10 USC § 379	Assignment of Coast Guard personnel to naval vessels for law enforcement purposes	Law enforcement detachments will be assigned to every appropriate surface vessel at sea in a drug interdiction area.
10 USC § 5013a	Secretary of the Navy: Powers with respect to the Coast Guard	Provides SECNAV with same powers as Secretary of Homeland Security when USCG is operating as a service in the Navy.
10 USC § 5061	Department of the Navy: Composition	Coast Guard is a DoN component when operating as a service in the Navy
14 USC § 1	Establishment of Coast Guard	Establishes the Coast Guard as a branch of the armed services "at all times."
14 USC § 2	Coast Guard Primary Duties	Coast Guard will, *inter alia*, maintain a state of readiness to function as a service in the Navy in time of war, including fulfillment of Maritime Defense Zone command responsibilities.
14 USC § 3	Coast Guard Relationship to Navy Department	If directed by Congress or the President, Coast Guard will operate as a service in the Navy; Transfer and use of appropriations, determinations of officer precedence, and awards to personnel authorized.
10 USC § 4	Secretary defined	"Secretary" means the Secretary of the respective department in which the Coast Guard is operating.
14 USC § 91	Safety of Naval Vessels	Authorizes control of any vessel in U.S. navigable waters in order to ensure the safety and security of any U.S. naval vessel.
14 USC § 145	Relations with Navy Department	SECNAV authorized to build Coast Guard vessels at Navy yards, receive Coast Guard members in any Navy school, provide Coast Guard personnel and their dependents Navy

		quarters, and detail Chaplains to the Coast Guard; exchanges of information, personnel, vessels, facilities and equipment authorized.
14 USC § 566	Department of Defense Consultation	Commandant shall make arrangements as appropriate for support in contracting and management of acquisitions; shall enter into MOA or MOU with ASN RD&A for exchange of technical assistance, use of technical expertise, and exchange of personnel.
33 USC § 381	Use of public vessels to suppress piracy	President is authorized to use public vessels to suppress piracy.
33 USC § 382	Seizure of piratical vessels	President may instruct commanders of public vessels to subdue, seize, take and send into port any armed vessel which attempted or committed piracy on any U.S. vessel, and to retake U.S. vessels or citizens captured on the high seas.
50 USC § 191	Regulation of anchorage & movement of vessels during national emergency	When national emergency declared, Secretary of the Department in which the Coast Guard is operating may make rules regarding anchorage and movement of vessels, and to guard against sabotage of vessels, ports and facilities.
50 USC § 191a	Transfer of powers to the SECNAV	When Coast Guard is operating as a service in the Navy, 50 USC § 191 powers are transferred to SECNAV.
50 USC § 3004	Definitions of military departments	"Department of the Navy" includes the Coast Guard when it is operating as part of the Navy.

Appendix A

Commonality Working Group: Mission/Plan of Action and Milestones

Permanent Joint Working Group

Mission

The U.S. Navy / U.S. Coast Guard Permanent Joint Working Group on Cutter Combat Systems Equipment was established in December 1988, and was formally chartered in March 1989 by the Navy/Coast Guard (NAVGARD) Board. The PJWG reviews and coordinates Navy Type / Navy Owned issues associated with CG combat weapons and C4 systems for both legacy and new cutter platforms, and provides recommendations to decision makers.

Recent Achievements

- The PJWG has been focused on 3 major issues over the last year:
  - Offshore Patrol Cutter's (OPC) combat systems suite.
  - OPC's NTNO C4 suite.
  - Sustainability of the NTNO systems aboard the 270' WMEC fleet.

Plan of Action and Milestones

The PJWG has played an active role regarding NTNO C4 and Combat Weapons Systems planning and coordination, and will continue to do so going forward. Of particular note, the PJWG will focus on supporting the fielding of new cutters – the National Response Cutter, Offshore Patrol Cutter, and Fast Response Cutter – and their associated NTNO systems. Furthermore, the PJWG will endeavor to maintain and/or improve the NTNO systems installed on the Coast Guard's legacy fleet. For example, the PJWG will oversee the completion of the 270' WMEC Combat Weapons Systems sustainability study, and will likely provide alternatives and recommendations to leadership based upon the results.

- Q2, FY14: Quarterly PJWG meeting.
- Q3, FY14: Quarterly PJWG meeting.
- Q4, FY14: Quarterly PJWG meeting.

Appendix B

Commonality Working Group: Mission/Plan of Action and Milestones

Small Boat Commonality Integrated Process Team

Mission

Share and compare boat requirements, capabilities, mission sets, and support systems of each Service and identify specific areas of potential commonality, cost savings, and best practices. (USN/USCG Small Boat Commonality Integrated Process Team Charter signed March 2011 and USN/USCG Joint Craft/Boat Capabilities and Acquisitions/Procurements MOA signed February 2012)

Recent Achievements

- Deployed a LEDET with a Cutter Boat – Over the Horizon (CB-OTH) onboard USS OAK HILL.

Plan of Action and Milestones

- Define goals/objectives of Sub-Integrated Process Team groups:
  - Procurement.
  - Lifecycle Management.
  - TTP.
- Q2, FY14: USN 7m/11m platform evaluation for CG Hook and Climb operations in support of overseas deployments for COCOMs.

Appendix C

Commonality Working Group: Mission/Plan of Action and Milestones

Naval Logistics Integration

Mission

The Naval Services will: (1) integrate policy, doctrine, business processes, technologies, and systems to optimize logistics performance in support of future operations. (2) Structure organizations and professional development to enhance support of naval expeditionary forces afloat and ashore. (3) Exploit opportunities to reduce operating costs.

- NLI outcomes and benefits include:
  - Improved logistics responsiveness and agility to better support the warfighter and increase resiliency.
  - Improved and sustained combat support readiness.
  - Improved efficiency through reduced logistics workload both afloat and ashore.
  - Reevaluation of naval logistics processes for more efficient use of resources.
  - Identify common processes between the Services to improve support to the warfighter, eliminate unnecessary duplication, and enhance sustainability.

Recent Achievements

- Transportation Exploitation Tool. (TET)
  - Identifies underutilized transportation opportunities.
  - Lessons needless duplication of resources.
- USMC and USCG use of Navy Priority Materiel Office. (PMO)
  - Identification and expediting of critical materiel operational units.
- Class II Individual Combat Clothing and Equipment Commonality.
  - Streamline RDT&E, acquisition, and supply chain management for common items
  - USMC responsible for the procurement of selected Class II items (individual ballistic protection systems, individual load bearing systems, flame resistant gear and cold weather gear) for all naval expeditionary forces.
- USCG use of Naval Working Uniform Type II in support of Naval Special Warfare.
- Littoral Combat Ship (LCS)/National Security Cutter (NSC) spares commonality.

- Identification of Common Systems.

- Commonality of Spares.

- Provisioning/Supply Support.

- Training.

- Common Logistics Solutions to Support Arctic Operations.

Plan of Action and Milestones

- Q2, FY14: Quarterly NLI Senior Board (O6)

- Q2, FY14: NLI Executive Board (1-2 Star)

- Q3, FY14: Quarterly NLI Senior Board (O6)

- Q4, FY14: Quarterly NLI Senior Board (O6)

- Q4, FY14/Q1, FY15: NLI Executive Board (1-2 Star)

- Q4, FY14/Q1, FY15: NLI Service Logistics Chiefs Board (3 Star USN, USMC, and USCG Service Logistics Chiefs)

- Q4, FY14: Submit FY15 NLI Annual Guidance

- TBD: Individual NLI IPT meet as required

Appendix D

Commonality Working Group: Mission/Plan of Action and Milestones

SSBN Transit Protection System (TPS)

Mission

- Provide a joint USN/USCG TPS decision forum.
  - Initially established to ensure effective implementation of TPS Program elements.
  - With acquisition nearing completion, mission has shifted to providing forum to discuss operation and sustainment issues.
  - Ensures smooth transition of all TPS program elements from acquisition to Final Operational Capability. (FOC)
  - Identifies and resolves issues associated with the TPS Program and operational plans as well as acquisition of TPS program elements.

Recent Achievements

- Dec 2012: Assessed alternate courses of action and a recommended TPS Course of Action (COA) to the TPS Flag Board.

Plan of Action and Milestones

- Military Construction (MILCON) P-993 is projected for a TPS Forward Operating Location at Port Angeles, Washington. The project is anticipated to be included in a future President's Budget. Milestones to date:
  - July 2012: Preliminary Design Authority
  - October 2013: Final Design Authority
- MILCON P-907 is the Bangor Pier and Landside project to provide piers and facilities for the TPS vessels at NBK Bangor. This project is not in the Program Objective Memorandum (POM). Phasing and funding alternatives are currently being explored.

Appendix E

Commonality Working Group: Mission/Plan of Action and Milestones

Interagency Operations Centers Working Group

Mission

Align Coast Guard and Navy Operational Planning and monitoring to optimize coordination and resource utilization in meeting security requirements.

Recent Achievements

- Working Group has not been active in recent years.

Plan of Action and Milestones

- Revalidate and scope work effort.

- Identify & familiarize WG team members.

- Q3, FY14: Draft new CG/Navy MOA for Port Security Operations and Coordination.

- Q4, FY14: Submit draft of MOA to National Fleet Board Members for review.

- Q4, FY14: Initiate inventory of common/required capability to support CG Navy coordination in the IOC environment.

- Q4, FY14: Submit inventory of common/required capability to support CG/Navy coordination in the IOC operating environment.

Appendix F

Commonality Working Group: Mission/Plan of Action and Milestones

Navy-Coast Guard Strategic Laydown Board

Mission

Coordinate strategic plans to station USCG units at USN facilities for greater than six months. This includes ships, aircraft and other units.

Recent Achievements

- Strategic Laydown (SLD) requests submitted:
  - 3 x Offshore Patrol Cutters to Naval Station Everett
  - 2 x Offshore Patrol Cutters to Naval Base San Diego
  - 6 x Fast Response Cutters to Naval Station Newport
  - 3 x Fast Response Cutters to Naval Base Guam
  - Aviation Assets to Naval Base Ventura County

- Organizational Change Requests (OCR) submitted:
  - 2 x Medium Endurance Cutters to JEB Little Creek
  - 3 x Fast Response Cutters to Naval Base Guam

Plan of Action and Milestones

- Q2, FY14: Quarterly Action Officer SLD meeting.

- Q2, FY14: Annual SLD meeting between CG-7 and N51.

- Q3, FY14: Quarterly Action Officer SLD meeting.

- Q4, FY14: Quarterly Action Officer SLD meeting.

Glossary

AA&E	Arms, Ammunition and Explosives
ADNS	Automated Digital Network System
AMLEP	African Maritime Law Enforcement Partnership
APS	Africa Partnership Station
ATG	Afloat Training Group
AUF	Airborne Use of Force
C2X	Composite Unit Training Exercise
C3	Command, Control, and Communications
C4I	Command, Control, Communications, Computers, and Intelligence
C4ISR	Command, Control, Communications, Computers, Intelligence, Surveillance, and Reconnaissance
CARAT	Cooperation Afloat Readiness and Training
CB-OTH	Cutter Boat - Over the Horizon
CCOP	Cryptologic Carry-On Program
CDLMS	Common Data Link Management System
CIT	Counter Illicit Trafficking
COA	Course of Action
CIWS	Close In Weapons System
DLA	Defense Logistics Agency
DLR	Depot Level Repairable
DMR	Defense Multi-Mode Radio
ESG	Escort Steering Group
E2E	End to End
FOC	Final Operational Capability
FRC	Coast Guard Fast Response Cutter
FRTP	Fleet Response Training Plan
FST	Fleet Synthetic Training
GCCS	Global Command and Control System
HVU	High Value Unit
IEW	Integration and Exercise Workshop
ILSP	Integrated Logistics Support Plan
IPT	Integrated Product Team
IWS	Integrated Warfare Systems
JHSV	Joint High Speed Vessel
JTFEX	Joint Task Force Exercise
LCS	Littoral Combat Ship
LEDET	Coast Guard Law Enforcement Detachment
LNO	Liaison Officer
MCC	Maritime Cryptologic Committee
MDA	Maritime Domain Awareness
MILCON	Military Construction

MIO	Maritime Interdiction Operations
MIPR	Military Interdepartmental Purchase Request
MOA	Memorandum of Agreement
MOU	Memorandum of Understanding
MUOS	Mobile User Objective System
NAVAIR	Naval Air Systems Command
NAVSEA	Naval Sea Systems Command
NAVSUP	Naval Supply Systems Command
NAVSSI	Navigation Sensor System Interface
NEC	Navy Enlisted Classification
NETC	Naval Education and Training Command
NLI	Naval Logistics Integration
NMDAP	National Maritime Domain Awareness Plan
NOC	Naval Operational Capabilities
NSC	Coast Guard National Security Cutter
NTCGO	Navy Type-Coast Guard Owned
NTNO	Navy Type-Navy Owned
NWU	Navy Working Uniform
OCR	Organizational Change Request
OIWG	Operational Integration Working Group
OMSI	Oceania Maritime Security Initiative
OPC	Coast Guard Offshore Patrol Cutter
PEO	Program Executive Office
PJWG	Permanent Joint Working Group
PMO	Priority Materiel Office
PMW	Program Manager Warfare
POM	Program Objective Memorandum
RB-M	Response Boat Medium
RB-S	Response Boat Small
RDT&E	Research, Development, Test and Evaluation
SATCOM	Satellite Communications
SFLC	Coast Guard Surface Forces Logistics Center
SLD	Strategic Laydown
SPAWAR	Space and naval Warfare Systems Command
TET	Transportation Exploitation Tool
TPS	Transit Protection System
TPST	Three Party Staff Talks
TPTS	Transit Protection Training System
TSC	Theater Security Cooperation
USFF	U.S. Fleet Forces Command
VBSS	Visit, Board, Search and Seizure
WMEC	Coast Guard Medium Endurance Cutter (Reliance and Famous Class)
WPB	Coast Guard Patrol Boat (Island Class)

www.ingramcontent.com/pod-product-compliance
Lightning Source LLC
Chambersburg PA
CBHW052018280526
45793CB00005B/1025